You're invited to embark on...

Adventures with the Universe

Change your life forever! Use this workbook to go on Adventures with the Universe and record your thoughts, beliefs and experiences.

For use in conjunction with the book
Adventures with the Universe by H. L. Savino.

In this journal you will practice the ABCs of abundance.

A stands for Allow

B stands for Believe

C stands for Clear

Remember:
Life can be easy. Relax, and let go. The Universe is waiting to catch you.

Intention:
I am now open to receiving all the good the Universe wants to send me. I allow abundance to flow in and change every part of my life for the better. Universe, please guide me on this adventure called life. Make it magical! I am relaxed and ready to receive.

Overview of the thirteen Adventures

Each week you'll learn a new Adventure. The weekly Adventures you'll embark on are meant to build on each other, so as you get more practice feeling abundant, you can move into more challenging ones.

If you fall in love with one of the Adventures, feel free to repeat it as often as you like.

Remember, every ninety days, you're a new you. Over the next ninety days, or three months, you can transform your life. Here's what we'll focus on each month:

Month One:
Clear.

You will learn how to clear any money or abundance blocks holding you back.

Month Two:
Believe.

You'll build belief in yourself and your infinite being, your connection to the Universe and the Source energy that makes life possible.

Month Three:
Allow.

You will learn to allow abundance and money to flow into your life. By the time you get to month three, you'll understand how easy it is to open up and receive everything you want.

Month One: Clear.

In this month we're going to work on clearing any money or abundance blocks holding you back.

Here are the four main categories of abundance blocks:

The "I'm not worthy/not good enough" block
The "money is evil" block
The "There's not enough to go around" block
The "More money and success isn't safe" block

Complete the simple quiz at www.adventureswiththeUniverse.com/quiz to find out what sort of money blocks you have. Then come back here and keep reading. The next few weeks' Adventures will help you remove these money blocks and lighten your mental load. You'll feel better instantly.

STOP PUTTING BRAKES ON YOUR OWN DESIRES

Week One

Adventure One

The Magic Spell

The Magic Spell has three steps. The first step is called the Gratitude Game. The second is called the Love list. By the time you're done with the first two steps, you'll be flying high on good feelings. Once you're feeling amazing, you complete step three and make a list of requests to the Universe. Finally, you turn your requests over to the Universe and release the white-knuckle grip on how abundance will come into your life.

THE MAGIC SPELL:

You will need:
- A journal and something to write with
- Note cards or extra paper
- A box to keep notes in

Steps to cast the spell:

Step One: The Gratitude Game

The fastest way to shift your frequency from scarcity to Abundance is to focus on what you already have and feel thankful.

How to play:

Write in your journal, "I'm so grateful for _____ because _____." Fill in the first blank with something you're grateful for that's nearby.

Example: "I'm so grateful for my green couch."

For the second blank, think of all the reasons why you're grateful for whatever you wrote in the first blank. There are probably tons of reasons, you've just never focused on them.

Example: "I'm so grateful for my green couch because I love the color. It looks nice in my living room. Plus, it's comfortable. I've wanted a couch like this ever since I saw the one my mom bought, and then a friend was getting rid of hers for $125! This couch is beautiful, durable, and cost me only $125. Win! Thank you, Universe!"

Choosing abundance over scarcity is a science-backed choice.

If you don't want to write down all of the reasons you're grateful, you can just write down one. But think through all the reasons and feel the feelings of gratitude well up within you. Feeling the feelings is the most important part of this game.

I am so grateful for _____

because _____

_____

I am so grateful for _____

because _____

_____

I am so grateful for _____

because _____

_____

I am so grateful for _____

because _____

_____

I am so grateful for _____

because _____

_____

I am so grateful for _____

because _____

_____

I am so grateful for _____

because _____

_____

I am so grateful for _____

because _____

_____

I am so grateful for _____

because _____

_____

Step two: The love list

This game is designed to get you feeling good as quickly as possible.

How to play:

In your journal, write out a list of 10 things you love most about your life. Write until you have a big smile on your face.

Here are some prompts

What do you love about your life?

What are your favorite people to hang out with? What do you love about them?

What are your favorite childhood memories?
Do you have pets? If so, what do you love about them?
Who are the most loving people in your life?
How do they make you feel?
Do you love the mountains or the ocean? List all the reasons why.
What is the most beautiful thing you've seen this year? Take a moment to appreciate it 100 fold.
What are your favorite flowers? Why?
What do you love most about the places you've lived?
What do you love most about nature? The outdoors? The wild places you've visited, or the closest parks and green spaces?
What do you love most about your body? From the top of your head to the tips of your toes, and all the organs in between.
What are your favorite foods?
What are your favorite types of clothes?
What are your favorite places to visit?
What are your favorite types of music? What are your favorite songs?
What are your favorite books, movies, TV shows, video or board or card games, plays, spectacles, things to do on a Friday night?

My love list:

Once you've filled a page or five, tune into your feelings. Do you feel good? Amplify that feeling. Dwell in it, if only for a few seconds. Stretch it out as long as you can. Feeling the feelings is the most important part of this step.

Reread your list and let the feelings of love and joy fill your heart. Intensify the feelings. Can you make those good feelings 10x stronger? 100x? 1000x?

Step three: Describe your Desires.

How to play:

Write down something you want to manifest. It can be big or small. You can write a whole "Want List" (like you'll do in Month Two, Adventure Five) or simply write down the first thing that comes to mind. There's no way to do this wrong. If you're having trouble thinking up what you want, ask the Universe to help you come up with something fun.

Here are some prompts

- Clothes you want to wear
- Foods you want to eat
- Gorgeous and fun stuff you want to own
- Items, big and small, you want to buy
- Places you want to travel
- People you want to meet
- Experiences you want to have
- Something small that would make life easier
- Something big that would make life grand
- Something delicious
- Something fun

Universe, please give me:

_____

_____

_____

_____

_____

_____

Step three: Release your Request.

How to play:

For this step, you'll need a box or container of some sort. I have a pretty one I ordered on Etsy inscribed with the words "Ask." I call it my 'Ask box'. But a sturdy shoebox works too.

Take your written request and fold it up and place it in your 'Ask box'. If I've listed out several things, I like to copy each entry separately onto note cards or nice stationery, then fold them up and put them in the box. This is a physical ritual to demonstrate to yourself that you are turning your wants and desires over to the Universe.

Once your request is in the box, it is no longer your responsibility. You've set the intention and it's the job of the Universe to do the rest. Relax. Everything you want is off your to do list. It's now the job of the Universe to deliver your requests in the best and most brilliant way possible. Prepared to be awed!!!!!

> The Universe is Gandalf on steroids, or the genie from Aladdin, but with unlimited power and unlimited wishes.

Week two
Adventure two

The Magic Spell

Start with gratitude:

I'm so grateful for _____

because _____

Now go on to Adventure Two!

Remember those money blocks you uncovered in this quiz?

www.adventureswiththeUniverse.com/quiz

If you haven't taken it, do it now! Then return here to go on this adventure and learn how to clear those blocks.
Let's review this sample list of abundance blocks. Check the box next to the statements that feel true to you.

The "I'm not worthy/good enough" block

If you've ever felt this way, check the box:

- ☐ I'm not worthy of earning lots of money.
- ☐ I'm not good enough to earn lots of money.
- ☐ I don't know enough to get started.
- ☐ I don't have anything to offer, I'm not smart or educated or important enough to be successful.
- ☐ I'm not ready. I need to know more before I can start.
- ☐ My course, product, book, art, or creation isn't ready. I need to add more/fix it/perfect it before it can go out into the world.
- ☐ There will never be enough money in my life. I can never earn enough, so why try?
- ☐ I'm doing/going to do it wrong. I'm not doing the right things.
- ☐ I'm going to mess up. I always mess up and make mistakes, so it's useless to try.
- ☐ Other people are better than I am.
- ☐ I'm a failure. I don't fit in with successful people; I'm not like them.
- ☐ People don't like me no matter what I do. People don't want me or what I have to offer.
- ☐ I'm a victim, I'm unloved, I'm unlovable, I'm broken.
- ☐ I've been cheated/will be cheated again, so it's useless to try.
- ☐ I'm too much, I'm overwhelming, I shine too brightly, I talk too much.
- ☐ I'm too over-the-top and weird, I'm too smart and being the smartest kid in class isn't safe.
- ☐ I've had money and lost it. I suck, I don't deserve more.
- ☐ I can't earn money because I'm not a man, I'm queer, I'm not white, I'm not American, I don't speak English as a first language, I don't look or talk or think like the rich people I know or see on TV. Other people deserve money and success, but not me.

- ☐ When I do have success, I minimize or apologize for it. I deflect compliments and qualify my success. I still don't know what I'm doing.
- ☐ I earned $100,000 but I spent so much on marketing.
- ☐ I'm successful now but it's just a fluke.
- ☐ I have to work hard to earn money, otherwise I don't deserve it.
- ☐ I'm not worthy if I'm not grinding it out, working 24/7, sleeping as little as possible. I don't deserve to have money flow to me easily and effortlessly. Earning lots of money has to be a struggle.

If you checked any of these boxes, then you have the "I'm not worthy/not good enough" block.

Truth: Your self-image is constricted and keeping you small. You think you have to be more—more educated, more skilled, more beautiful, more organized, more put-together, more hard working, older, thinner, healthier, younger, smarter, faster, hungrier… the list goes on and on!

You are worthy as you are. You deserve money now. Once you clear this block you'll see yourself as someone worthy of all the riches you could ever want.

The "money is evil" block

If you've ever felt this way, check the box:

- ☐ Money corrupts people.
- ☐ Rich people are evil.
- ☐ Being poor means I'm holy/more spiritual/closer to God.
- ☐ Poverty is noble.
- ☐ Money is the root of all evil.
- ☐ If I have more money, I won't be a good person.
- ☐ Money is dirty–i.e., physical bills and coins are unclean, and taint my conception of money as a whole.
- ☐ The only way to get more money is to scam someone or embrace unethical practices. I don't want to compromise my ethics, so I can only earn a limited amount. Any more than that means I'm a bad person.
- ☐ Earning money doing what I love–writing books, creating art or beautiful products, teaching, coaching or serving people–is selling out.
- ☐ I love helping people, but if I charge money for it, I'm hurting the people I want to help.
- ☐ People in my profession should be poor. Artists should starve.
- ☐ Teachers shouldn't be able to pay their bills. Otherwise they're not doing all they can to serve humanity.
- ☐ It's wrong to have more than what I need.
- ☐ Life is meant to be hard and test my perseverance. Ease and joy mean I'm not growing spiritually.
- ☐ To truly live my calling, I have to be a martyr.

If you checked any of these boxes then you have the "money is evil" block.

Truth: Abundance is divine. Money isn't evil, but a tool like a hammer. You can use it for good or otherwise. Rich people are just people. Having more money doesn't make you better than anyone else, and neither does being poor.

I grew up learning "The love of money is the root of all evil," and when I asked a Bible teacher for more clarification, they explained the term "love of money" was called "Mammon," which means "greed." Greed comes from a feeling of lack, a grasping, needy sense that there can 'never be enough.' The opposite of greed is unlimited abundance. "You can't serve God and Mammon" makes sense because God is abundance, and Mammon is the opposite of abundance.

You deserve to have all you want or need, regardless of your profession. You can earn money by serving others. And when you embrace abundance, you're helping others even more. It's healthy for people to pay for goods or services that delight them. Release these lies to allow more money into your life.

The "There's not enough to go around" block

If you've ever felt this way, check the box:

- ☐ There's a limited amount of money/abundance and if I get more, I'm taking from others.
- ☐ There's not enough money, health, water, air, happiness, caviar or land to go around.
- ☐ Wanting more is selfish.
- ☐ It's okay to want things, but not too much, because then I'm stealing from others. I deserve a little bit but not more.
- ☐ There's no such thing as unlimited abundance.
- ☐ I can't have it all.
- ☐ I can't afford that.
- ☐ I have to save every penny.
- ☐ No matter what I do, I can't get ahead.
- ☐ I'll always be in debt.
- ☐ I can only earn money one way.
- ☐ I can only earn money working a job. I can't do what I love and earn millions.
- ☐ Not everyone can be a millionaire.
- ☐ Money doesn't grow on trees—even though it is literally paper, and where do you think paper comes from, Dad?
- ☐ There's a limited number of customers/clients and one day I'll run out of people to sell to and my business will have to close.
- ☐ I can make a bunch of money but then a karmic rubber band will snap and I'll be hurled back into debt.

If you checked any of these boxes then you have the "There's not enough to go around" block.

Truth: the Universe and abundance has no limits! When we create from a place of unlimited potential, we unlock more riches for everyone. You're not taking a bigger slice of the pie—you're growing the size of the whole pie! Think of the inventions that make everyone's lives better—from surgeries to solar panels, Shakespeare's plays, Beethoven's symphonies and Botticelli's paintings. These inventions and creations inspire the next wave of inventions and art like the internet and Ai, N.K Jemison novels and Tracy Chapman's albums.

The "More money and success isn't safe" block

You have this block if you believe the lie that…

- [ ] If I earn more money, I'll become a target. People will come out of the woodwork to ask for a handout. My family will guilt me into financing their lifestyle. I'll never have any peace!
- [ ] I'll be persecuted and made an example of if I get too wealthy/too successful. People will criticize me publicly.
- [ ] If I'm more successful and more visible, there will be so much pressure. I can never make a mistake.
- [ ] Change is scary, big numbers are scary, the only way I'll be safe is if things stay the same.
- [ ] It's scary to have large amounts in my checking or savings account.
- [ ] I'm not sure if I can handle it.
- [ ] I'm not good with money.
- [ ] I have to save every penny. Disaster and bankruptcy is right around the corner. At any minute, I could lose it all.
- [ ] Easy come, easy go.
- [ ] If I earn more money, I'll have to pay more in taxes, so I better limit my earnings to only pay the amount of taxes I'm familiar and comfortable with.
- [ ] The money will come but then I'll lose it right away, and it will devastate me. It's better to avoid disappointment and not even try.
- [ ] I can't get more customers/clients/sell more because then I'll have more refunds/complaints/negative reviews.
- [ ] If I sell to people, they'll think I'm using them.
- [ ] If I hire people, they'll hate me because I'm the boss.
- [ ] Employees/renters/customers are always out to cheat me. They want a handout, they're not willing to pay.
- [ ] It's not safe for me to stand out or shine. It is dangerous for me to be myself or be too different or make more money than the richest person I know.
- [ ] If I put myself out there to sell something or be successful, I'll look like a fool. People will judge me. I'll be publicly humiliated.

- [ ] If I make more money than my friends and family, they'll feel bad.
- [ ] My success will make them feel like a failure and they'll be sad or angry, they will shun, reject and abandon me.
- [ ] I can't make more money than my parents, mentor or the most successful person I know. It would be disrespectful.
- [ ] It's better to be nice than successful. I can't be both.
- [ ] I can't handle more money–I have bad money habits and more money will only lead to disaster. How will I manage it all?
- [ ] The thought of having a lot of money in my bank account is intimidating.
- [ ] If I shine too bright or work too hard, I'll burn out.
- [ ] I've never been successful or earned a lot of money before and it feels scary.
- [ ] I tell myself, "I don't know what to do next. I don't know how to make more money." because it's easier to stop myself from thinking up ways to make more money than face my fears.

If you checked any of these boxes then you have the "More money and success isn't safe" block.

Truth: Fear holds you back, because it's trying to keep you safe. Your brain wants you to stay in your comfort zone where things are familiar.
In primal times, that meant staying close to your campfire and cave, and not venturing out into the forest where a sabertooth tiger might eat you. The unknown is scary, and the fear wants to keep you in a tight,
confined space.

In the months to come, you will make wealth and success more familiar. You will normalize having bigger and bigger numbers in your bank
account. What was once unknown and scary will become old hat. I used to think having over $1000 in my bank account was a big deal. Now I have tens of thousands of dollars in my business bank account—and if it dips, I make money moves and decisions to top it up to the proper amount. In
the following chapters, I'll cover the exact methods I used to 10x my funds. Don't worry, earning and having more money can be easy and effortless.

Follow the steps of each adventure and normalize larger and larger
amounts of money. Soon, you will know the truth: you don't need the fear. You are safe in the arms of the Universe.

Are you ready to exhume your money blocks and set them on fire?

Repeat after me:

"I now clear anything that's blocking the flow of money into my life."

Repeat this statement until you feel lighter. Then, go and do something that feels good. Take a walk or a nap or a relaxing bath. I like to take a shower and repeat the statement and imagine all my old beliefs washing away.

You accepted these beliefs and put them in place to keep you safe. You are an infinite, powerful being and you can banish these beliefs with a word or a thought.

If you want more help clearing your Abundance blocks, join me and my friend Renee Rose in the Money Magic Membership Course. We have regular calls to energetically clear abundance blocks.

I'm going to make a statement, and you're going to get still and pay attention to how it makes you feel.

Money comes easily and effortlessly.

Okay, now, how do you feel? Repeat the statement in your head. Does it feel light and easy? Or is there a part of you that immediately rejects it? When you start to pay attention, you might hear a rebuttal. I call this the "negative echo."

When I got quiet and listened, I realized every time I spoke positively about money, my brain resisted in the form of a negative echo. That resistance was what I truly believed, and that belief was blocking money from flowing into my life.

Here are a few examples of the negative echo:

Money comes easily and effortlessly.

<negative echo> "No, it doesn't."

Money comes easily and effortlessly. <negative echo> "Maybe if you're a crook!"

Money comes easily and effortlessly.

<negative echo> "Easy come, easy go."

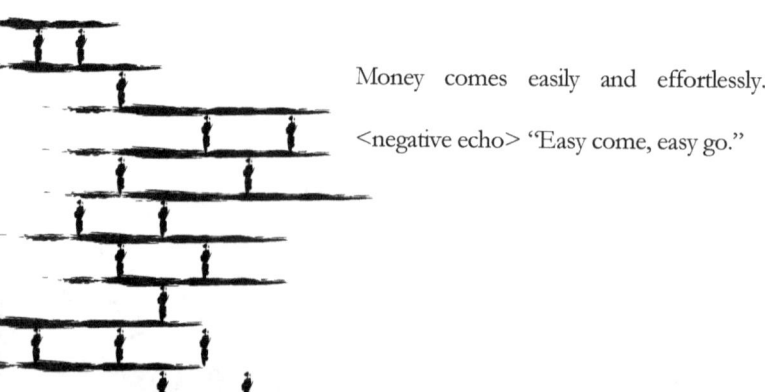

You might hear something different in rebuttal, but pay attention. If it's negative, it's a money block. If it feels heavy or icky, it's resistance to abundance. Resistance is something you create because you feel unworthy of what you want. It's a sign you have a money block that you put in place to hold yourself back. No one's stopping you but yourself.

Your blocks were trying to protect you. But you don't need them anymore, so we're going to clear them.

The adventures in the coming weeks are designed to clear money blocks. But for fast relief now, say to yourself:

"I now clear anything that's blocking the flow of money into my life."

You can clear your beliefs over and over. Let's do it now! I'm going to make a statement about money, and you're going to hear the negative echo and clear it. Do this as many times as it takes to feel relief.

Money comes easily and effortlessly.

<negative echo>

"I clear that belief about money."

I can have all the money I want. Every day it flows into my life.

<negative echo>

"I clear that belief about money."

I love money.

\<negative echo\>

"I clear that belief, and any other belief that's blocking the flow of money into my life."

I can have what I want

\<negative echo\>

"I clear that belief, and any other belief that's blocking the flow of money into my life."

I can afford it

\<negative echo\>

"I clear that belief, and any other belief that's blocking the flow of money into my life."

Did you clear all the resistance that came up when you read those statements? If you're overwhelmed, you might put this book down, and try again later this week. You might have a lot of crud to clear.

If you feel the relief, enjoy the feeling. Be grateful for it. And relax knowing from now on, when negative feelings about money arrive, you can quickly clear them.

Over the next few weeks, you're going to learn many ways to clear your money blocks. Some will work for your situation better than others. But we've been doing a lot of work here, so give yourself a hug and go do something to pamper yourself.

Bonus question to journal about: What other blocks do I have and how do they stop me?

_____

_____

_____

_____

_____

_____

_____

_____

_____

_____

_____

_____

_____

_____

_____

_____

_____

_____

_____

_____

_____

_____

_____

_____

Ask the Universe to give you the answer and help you clear the blocks away.

Week three
Adventure three

Start with gratitude:

I'm so grateful for _____

because _____

Start with gratitude:

I'm so grateful for _____

because _____

Now go on Adventure three!

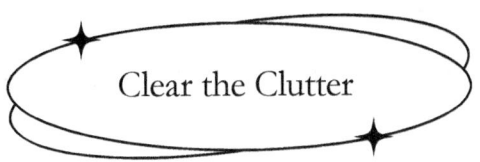

Clear the Clutter

Step one: Clear the clutter

Step two: Visualize your home as you like it. Dwell on a sense of calm and peace, clean and easy to navigate, everywhere you look is something you love! Invite the Universe to help you design the perfect space in your mind, and connect you with the feelings of freedom, peace and wealth.

What would it take for you to love the space you're in?

_____
_____
_____
_____
_____
_____
_____
_____
_____
_____
_____
_____
_____
_____
_____
_____
_____
_____

What ideas do you have to transform your space into a home you love?

Step three: Clear the clutter in your purse or wallet.

If you were a millionaire, what sort of bag would you carry? Upgrade the wallet or purse you're carrying to a beautiful one that makes you feel good.

List your dream purse/wallet upgrades here:

_____
_____
_____
_____
_____
_____
_____
_____
_____
_____
_____
_____
_____
_____
_____
_____
_____
_____

Universe, please bring me the perfect bag, purse, or wallet.

Step four: Clear the clutter out of your home.

- Get three containers or bags. One for trash, one for storage, the other for donating. Go through your house and clean the clutter. Trash goes into the trash. Broken and stained items are trash.
- Most items you haven't used for over a year are either trash or should be donated. If you cannot bring yourself up to trash or give away an item, but you are done with it, put it into storage. In a few months, return to the storage box and see if you can let it go.
- Consider hiring a service to help you, or bartering with a friend to make the work more fun.

Our physical world reflects our mental world.

Step Five: Clear the Digital Clutter.

- TV and radio: Turn off your TV. Turn off the radio.
- Email: search the word "unsubscribe" and remove yourself from any newsletter that's not serving you.
- Turn off all website and app notifications on your browser and phone.
- Social media: Unfollow, unfriend, or downright block negative people from your newsfeed and your life.
- If social media leaves you grouchy, delete or pause your account and remove the apps from your phone.
- Consider leaving your phone in a box or drawer a few hours of the day.

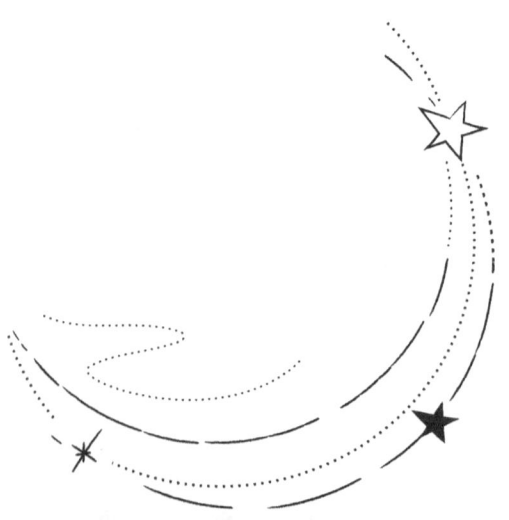

Step six: Clear the Clutter: Bills

Universe, please transform my finances and make room for my riches.

List any ideas/nudges you have on decluttering your bank account:

_____
_____
_____
_____
_____
_____
_____
_____
_____
_____
_____
_____
_____
_____
_____
_____
_____
_____

If any negative feelings like guilt or shame come up, clear them away.

"I now clear away my feelings about my bills and bank account."

Step Seven: Give yourself a hug, pat yourself, and go take a nap. The act of decluttering is powerful but can bring up a lot of gunky feelings. It's okay to go slowly and get help.

Universe, please help me declutter my life and make room for more abundance. And please make the process EASY and MAGICAL.

List any ideas/nudges you have on decluttering your life:

_____
_____
_____
_____
_____
_____
_____
_____
_____
_____
_____
_____
_____
_____
_____
_____
_____
_____
_____

Week four
Adventure four

Congratulations! You've spent the better part of a month exhuming your money blocks and setting them on fire. This week you're going to shed more mental and emotional burdens so you can make space for amazing riches to pour into your life.

Start with gratitude:

I'm so grateful for   because

_____

_____

Now go on Adventure four!

Step one: cut the cords

How to play:

Relax into a comfy position with some relaxing music playing, like the Reiki list on Spotify. Imagine one of your friends or family members in front of you, with a glowing gold thread connecting you to them. Sometimes the cord is thick like steel thread. Sometimes it's gossamer thin, no more substantial than a spiderweb.

Pretend one end of the cord is velcroed to your heart space, and peel it away. Tug it off the other person, too. You can imagine cutting the cord between you first using scissors or a machete, but make sure you unhook the thread from both you and them so it doesn't re-form.

Repeat "I clear my relations with <*name of the person*>."
Remember, this exercise doesn't harm you or the other person. Instead, it frees you both from an old pattern so you can reconnect on new, loving terms.

Bonus: set a reminder in your calendar to do this meditation on the first of every month.

Step two: list people who've wronged you

_____

_____

_____

_____

_____

_____

Write: "I now forgive _name of person_ and release all unforgiveness I've been hanging onto."

If you can't forgive them, ask the Universe to forgive them for you.

"Please forgive _____ for me and release all unforgiveness from my soul and body."

_____

_____

_____

_____

_____

Repeat this over and over again until you feel light and free.

Bonus: Think of the best possible thing that could happen to the people you need to forgive and wish that for them. This is so powerful. You immediately become bigger than the situation. And you reap what you sow, so any good thing you wish for another, you're actually wishing for yourself. Let Karma take care of avenging you, and sow only good things so you can reap the same.

Step three: Forgive yourself.

List ways you've harmed yourself

_____
_____
_____
_____
_____

I now forgive myself for any and every harm or hurt I've inflicted on myself. I release all grudges or unforgiveness towards myself. I understand that in the past, I was doing my best. I now clear all judgements and criticism of myself I've been holding onto. I clear my negative opinions and beliefs of myself.

_____
_____
_____
_____
_____

Universe, please help me forgive myself and release all unforgiveness from my soul and body.

Step four: Choose to love yourself

What do you love about yourself?

_____
_____
_____
_____
_____
_____
_____
_____
_____
_____
_____
_____
_____
_____
_____
_____
_____
_____
_____
_____
_____
_____
_____
_____

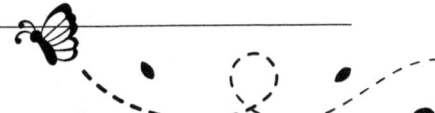

What is awesome and unique about you?

_____
_____
_____
_____
_____
_____
_____
_____
_____
_____
_____
_____
_____
_____
_____
_____
_____
_____
_____
_____
_____
_____
_____
_____
_____
_____
_____
_____

What are ways you can honor and respect yourself more deeply?

"I choose myself now."

Month Two: believe.

Week five
Adventure five

Start with gratitude:

I'm so grateful for _____

because _____

Now go on Adventure five!

Step One: Write out a list of what you want in this season of your life—an item, a job, an opportunity, an amount of money. Write it as you want to see it happen in your life.

Example:

- I want strong and health hips that feel good whether I'm walking, standing, sitting, or resting
- I want my business to earn 7 million this year
- I want a freshly renovated second floor of our house, with nice wood floors and beautiful rugs, new paint and decorations to make a cozy hygge space
- I want a fabulous trip to Tuscany where everything goes smoothly and I'm able to see lots of art and stunning sights, and eat lots of pasta and gelato. A trip of a lifetime!

Prompts:

Clothes you want to wear
Foods you want to eat
Gorgeous and fun stuff you want to own
Items, big and small, you want to buy
Places you want to travel
People you want to meet
Experiences you want to have
How you want to feel achieving your goals

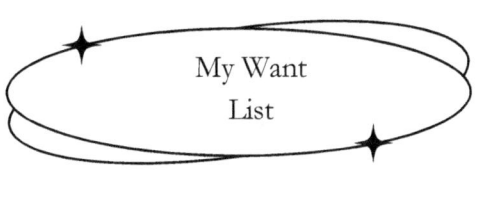

My Want List

Reread your list and imagine it all coming into your life until you feel giddy. How will you feel when all the things you want appear in your life like magic?

The Complain Game

How to play:

If you're feeling stuck imagining what you want, think of all the things you don't want. Then write out the opposite scenario of what you're hating:

_____
_____
_____
_____

Reread your list and imagine it all coming into your life until you feel giddy.

How will you feel when all the things you want appear in your life like magic?

_____
_____
_____
_____

Examples: Abundant, Free, Excited, Wonderful, Safe, Loved, Ecstatic, Powerful, Content, Supported, Magical, Victorious

Dwell on these feelings. Feel them now. Intensify them until your body vibrates with the giddy sensation. Pump your fist into the air. Get up and dance! What you want is flying towards you so feel the feelings now.

Step 2: Window shopping

As you go about your day, your world is the Universe's magical department store, a menu of delights you get to order from. You can order as much or as little as you like. Every time you see something you want, tell yourself "I can afford that."

Go for a walk past your favorite stores. Every time you see something you want, say "I can afford that!"

Online, browse your favorite shopping websites and put items on your wishlist or in your cart.

Go to realtor open houses or car lots. And tell yourself:

I can afford that!

I can afford that!

I can afford that!

List some fun things you've seen today that gave you a chance to affirm "I can afford that!"

___

If you hear a negative echo pop up— clear that rebuttal away. "I now clear my feelings and beliefs about money."

I can afford that!

<negative echo> "No, I can't."

"I now clear my feelings and beliefs about money."

Step 3: "I'll have some of that please!"

How to play:

Whenever you see someone who has what you want or enjoying success you'd love to have, bless and praise them. Say: "I bless and praise you."
If you don't like the word "bless" you can say "affirm" instead. You don't have to say it to them, just say it under your breath:

I bless and praise you.

I bless and praise you.

I bless and praise you.

And then tell the Universe, "I'll have some of that, please!"

List examples of who, what, where and why is living out your dream life now:

___

"I'll have some of that too, please!"

If any jealous feelings come up, remember that the only reason you feel negative is because you're affirming both: "I want what they have" and "I don't believe I can have it." Clear this negative belief away.

"I want what they have and I deserve to have it, too."

List any abundance blocks or "negative echoes" that come up:

_____
_____
_____
_____
_____
_____
_____
_____
_____
_____
_____
_____
_____
_____
_____
_____
_____
_____
_____

Universe, please clear these jealous feelings away and replace it with a belief that I can have what others are having!!

Week six
Adventure six

Start with gratitude:

I'm so grateful for _____

because _____

Start with gratitude:

I'm so grateful for _____

because _____

Now go on Adventure six!

Step One: Create a dream board

What images could you gather to give you the feelings of having your want list now?

When you look at the images you've gathered for a dream board, how do you feel?

_____
_____
_____
_____
_____
_____
_____
_____
_____
_____
_____
_____
_____
_____
_____
_____
_____

If any jealousy or feelings of "I can't afford that/I can't have that" come up, clear them away.

"I now clear anything that's blocking what I want from coming into my life."

Week seven
Adventure seven

Start with gratitude:

I'm so grateful for _____

because _____

Start with gratitude:

I'm so grateful for _____

because _____

Now go on Adventure seven!

What were you were petrified to try only a few months, years, or decades ago? Examples: Driving a car, going to kindergarten, starting your dream business

List them now:

_____
_____
_____
_____
_____
_____
_____
_____
_____
_____
_____
_____
_____
_____
_____
_____
_____
_____

If any jealousy or feelings of "I can't afford that/I can't have that" come up, clear them away.

"I now clear anything that's blocking what I want from coming into my life."

Step 1: Create Your Dream Bank Account

How to play:

Grab a bank statement, either a physical print out or digital one. Write in a new total.

What amounts would you like to see in your bank accounts?

I now have… in my bank account:

_____
_____
_____
_____
_____

What about your investment accounts?

_____
_____
_____
_____

What feelings come up when you look at these numbers and imagine them in your accounts?

_____
_____
_____
_____

"Anything that's blocking the flow of money into my accounts, I now destroy and uncreate it now."

Step Two: Abundance Tracker

Track the abundance flowing into your life. Create an excel spreadsheet or download one at https://geni.us/abundancetracker

What money has flowed into your life today? Include deposits in your bank account and value of gifts/discounts you've received:

_____
_____
_____
_____
_____
_____
_____
_____
_____
_____
_____
_____
_____
_____
_____
_____
_____
_____
_____
_____

Step three: Create Your Dream Bills

What are the amounts of your bills? Write them out and write a number ten times the amount beside it.

Bills	Money received

Imagine paying your bills and having plenty of extra money left over. Feel grateful for the money. If you feel yucky, repeat after me:

"I clear my beliefs about my bank account."
"I clear my beliefs about my checkbook."
"I clear my beliefs about my debt."
"I clear my beliefs about bills."

Write out all the reasons you're grateful for your bills:
Example: I'm so grateful for my water bill, because I love taking hot showers!

_____
_____
_____
_____
_____
_____
_____
_____
_____
_____
_____
_____
_____
_____
_____
_____
_____

"Every dollar I spend comes back to me one hundred fold."

Imagine if every dollar you spent returned to you with ninety-nine of its best buddies. How awesome would that feel? Feel into this feeling.

Week eight
Adventure eight

Now go on Adventure eight!

Step 1: Tiny Upgrades

Take $10-20 and go buy some small items that will make your life instantly better.

Here are some ideas of what to buy:

- New pens
- A new mug
- A song streaming service
- Cute pillows
- Treat yourself to coffee, lunch, and/or dessert
- A new toothbrush.
  Hint: You probably have a new one in a drawer under your bathroom sink. Time to break it out!

What small upgrades can you implement today?

_____
_____
_____
_____
_____
_____
_____
_____
_____
_____
_____
_____

The moment you buy the item, affirm over and over: "I can afford it! I can afford it!"

More upgrading ideas:

When you upgrade, the underlying message is "I am worth nice things. I trust I will have the money to buy what I need in the future." So subtle, but it sends a powerful message to the Universe.

Step Two: Lifestyle Upgrades 2.0

How to play:

Take $20-100 and invest in an upgrade to your life.
- Here are some ideas:
- Upgrade your bath mats and shower curtain.
- Buy excellent coffee and tea.
- A new art piece that catches your eye at a farmer's market.
- Splurge lunch or dinner out by yourself or with a loved one. You can still go on dream dates if you're single——take yourself!
- Treat yourself to a movie out.
  Hire someone to mow your lawn or fix a broken towel rack - a small job you've been putting off.
- Buy yourself nice new pillows and sheets. Or towels. And a silk pillowcase!
- Upgrade your phone charger.
- Decorate with a new plant.
- Buy yourself fresh flowers.
  If any negative feelings arise, clear them.

Universe, please help me upgrade until I'm living my dream life, surrounded by things I love. And please make the process fun!

Month three: allow.

Week nine
Adventure nine

Start with gratitude:

I'm so grateful for _____

because _____

Now go on Adventure nine!

Step 1: Nap and grow rich

How to play:

- Try an affirmation on my Youtube Channel or in my Money Magic Membership course with Renee Rose
Put on soothing music, close your eyes and imagine money raining into your life. Imagine it piling up all around you. You only have to reach out and pick some up.

- Meditation 3
  _____

- Meditation 4
  _____

- Meditation 5
  _____

- Meditation 6
  _____

- Meditation 7
  _____

What meditation resonated most with you?
_____
_____
_____
_____
_____
_____
_____
_____
_____

Reflect on anything that came up during the meditations:

Step Two: Affirmations

How to play:

Repeat the words "Wealth and success" silently or out loud. Allow the pleasant images those two words conjure up to float around in your head.

Try it now:

Wealth and success.

Wealth and success.

Wealth and success.

Step Three: MOAR Affirmations

Repeat the following affirmations. If you hear a negative echo, say "I now clear my beliefs about money."

I now clear my beliefs about money.

I love abundance.

Abundance is all around.

I'm surrounded by wealth and success.

I am open to receiving abundance.

I am meant to enjoy life.

I am worthy.

I am open to living in abundance.

Abundance is pouring into my life now.

My life is full of wealth and success.

I am gratefully receiving abundance.

I enjoy life.

I am living my best life now.

I am worthy.

I am wealthy.

I love money.

I have so much money.

Money pours into my life easily.

I have all the money I need.

I am so grateful for all the money I am receiving.

I love being wealthy.

I love earning money.

I easily earn money.

People give me things all the time.

I am open to receiving all good things.

I love having money.

I love saving money.

I love investing money.

I love organizing my money.

I am a brilliant money manager.

I have so much money.

I always have the money I need.

It's safe for me to be wealthy.

Money comes to me easily and effortlessly.

I am so grateful for my wealth.

I am so grateful for my success.

I am so grateful for my life.

I am living in abundance.

Everyone and everything prospers me now!

Week ten
Adventure ten

Start with gratitude:

I'm so grateful for _____ because

_____

Now go on Adventure ten!

Step 1: Become a Scholar of Abundance

How to play:

Go to the library or splurge and buy some of the following books. I prefer books on audio because I listen to them when I'm in the car. Here are some of my favorites:

- *The Secret and The Power* by Rhonda Byrne
- *Beyond Positive Thinking* by Dr. Robert Anthony
- *Ask and it is Given* by Abraham Hicks
- *You are A Badass* by Jen Sincero
- *The Success Principles* by Jack Canfield
- *Get Rich, Lucky Bitch* by Denise Duffield-Thomas
- *We Should all be Millionaires* by Rachel Rodgers
- *Write to Riches* by Renee Rose

Thoughts on these books or your favorite inspirational resources:

_____
_____
_____
_____
_____
_____
_____
_____
_____
_____
_____
_____
_____
_____

Step 2: Find your Models

How to play:

Find the people who are crushing it in the areas you want success. People who are living a life you'd love to live.

List people who inspire you to live your dreams:

_____
_____
_____
_____
_____
_____
_____
_____
_____
_____
_____
_____
_____
_____
_____
_____
_____
_____

Universe, please send me great role models so I can believe my dream life is possible!

Step Three: Find Your Tribe

How to play:

Find a community to support your new lifestyle. If you want to be a writer, join a writing group on Facebook. If you want to hike more, join a hiking Meetup.com group. If you want to be better at budgeting, find a free Facebook group and connect with people focused on the same goal.

Ideas on where to find your tribe:

_____
_____
_____
_____
_____
_____
_____
_____
_____
_____
_____
_____
_____
_____
_____

Universe, please help me find a supportive community who will cheer me on as I reach for my goals!

More brainstorming on where to find your tribe:

_____
_____
_____
_____
_____
_____
_____
_____
_____
_____
_____
_____
_____
_____
_____
_____
_____
_____
_____
_____

If you want to surround yourself with people focusing on Abundance, I recommend joining th I run it with my good friend and co-author, Renee Rose. Together we teach you more ways to clear your abundance blocks–and we have regular live calls you can join where we use our spiritual gifts to energetically clear the group's abundance blocks. With the course, you get access to a community where we record our manifesting successes and root for each other!

Week eleven
Adventure eleven

I am so grateful for _____

because _____

_____

Now go on Adventure eleven!

Step One:

Give money

How to play:

Today, find ways to give a little extra money.
Ways to give money:
- Tip extravagantly.
- Leave a $5 or $10 bill with a post-it note that says something like: "This money is for you."
- Send money anonymously to someone in need.
- Donate money to your favorite charity.
- Gift Five:

  _____

- Gift Six:

  _____

- Gift Seven:

  _____

Brainstorm on ways you can give money:

_____
_____
_____
_____
_____

This game smashes the belief "rich people are evil" to smithereens. You're proving to yourself that if you have tons of money, you'd be able to give more. You'd be able to bless the world in so many extra ways. Who better to be wealthy than you?

Step Two:

Give Value

How to play:

- Whatever you sow, you reap.
- Focus on giving extra value in your job, business or life!
Ideas:
- If you are an author or creator, give something you made away. (As an author, I give away a lot of free books.)
- If you're an employee, give extra—--go above and beyond your job description today.
- If you're a stay- at- home parent, plan something special for your kids, like a scavenger hunt or a favorite meal.
- Pick flowers and arrange them into a beautiful display.
- Call a friend and sing them a song to cheer them up.
- Lend a helping hand.
- Write one thank you note—---or several!
- Give kindness, give compliments, give love, give your time. And feel good.
- Brainstorm ways you can give more value

_____
_____
_____
_____
_____
_____

Universe, please give me ideas on how to give more value. Make it easy and fun!

Week twelve
Adventure twelve

Start with gratitude:

I'm so grateful for _____

because _____

Now go on Adventure twelve!

Step One: Millionaire Day

How to play:

Plan a "Millionaire Day." What would your life be like if you had earned a million dollars last year, and were guaranteed to earn a million this year and for the rest of your life? Write out your perfect day. Then, take a day off and indulge in a "staycation." Live into your perfect day as much as possible.

What would you do when you wake up?

_____
_____
_____
_____
_____
_____
_____

What would you eat or drink?

_____
_____
_____
_____
_____
_____
_____

Where would you go?

___

What would you buy?

___

What music would you listen to?

___

Who would you hang out with?

How else can you make your Millionaire Day special?

Every moment you can, be still and feel into the fact that this is your life now. Feel the feelings of having your dream life now.

Week thirteen
Adventure thirteen

Start with gratitude:

I'm so grateful for _____

because _____

Now go on Adventure thirteen!

Step One: Play the Gratitude Game with money:

How much money came into your life before you knew what money was? Make a list of ways abundance made it into your life when you were a child. Did someone buy you clothes? Food? Shelter? Did you have access to running water?

List these ways you dwelt in abundance even when you were a baby, and feel the feelings of gratitude.

Shelter:

_____
_____
_____
_____
_____
_____
_____

Clothing you loved:

_____
_____
_____
_____
_____
_____
_____

Shelter:

___

Clothing you loved:

___

Toys:

Education:

___

___

___

___

___

___

___

Trips:

___

___

___

___

___

___

___

Priceless items--love, friends, family, memories, puppy dogs, great night's sleep, health, blue sky, fresh air, sunlight and running water!

___

___

___

___

How wealthy were you? It's time to say thank you and realize your life has ALWAYS been abundant!!!!

Be grateful for the abundance the Earth gives us:

- Did you ever enjoy a blue sky? A rainstorm? A snow day? A beach day?
- Did you ever sit under a tree and find relief in the shade?
- Did you ever cuddle a pet? Or watch a bird splash in a puddle?

Chronicle all the ways abundance and money showed up in your life, without you even realizing it. Every sip of water you took, every cut that healed, every molecule of oxygen: take a moment to be grateful for it all.

_____
_____
_____
_____
_____
_____
_____
_____
_____
_____
_____
_____
_____
_____

Step Two: Write a letter to money.

Apologize for the cruel ways you've treated it or pushed it out of your life. Ask it to flow into your life. Outline the ways you're going to make space for it. Ask it to stick around in your bank accounts and invite more of its friends to party!

How have you been treating your friend "Money"?

Dear Money,

_____
_____
_____
_____
_____
_____
_____
_____
_____
_____
_____
_____
_____
_____
_____
_____
_____
_____

Put the letter in your Ask box or fold it up and burn it.

"I now release my relationship with money to the Universe."

Step Three: Go on a date with money.

Take a walk and point out all the things money can buy. Acknowledge all the free oxygen and sunlight you enjoy. Revisit the "Wealth and Success" affirmation outlined in Step Two of Adventure nine. Repeat a mini portion of your "Millionaire Day" and dwell on how money makes it possible. Every time you make a purchase, thank the money you spend and invite it to
visit you again.

Ideas for your date with money:
_____
_____
_____
_____
_____
_____
_____
_____
_____
_____
_____
_____
_____
_____
_____
_____
_____
_____
_____

Universe, please teach me more ways to love money and make space for it!

Step Four: (Optional)

Print out a picture of a hottie and write "The Universe is My Sugar Daddy." Place it in your purse, wallet or make like a '90s kid and hang it up as a poster over your bed.

Congratulations! You completed 13 Adventures with the Universe!

Free Resources:

- Free Abundance blocks quiz: https://adventureswiththeUniverse.com/quiz/
- The Adventures with the Universe Facebook group

- My website: www.leesavino.com/adventures
  Free meditations on my Youtube Channel
- Remember to take the Abundance blocks quiz: https://adventureswiththeUniverse.com/quiz/.
- It's the first step to blasting through the negative beliefs that hold you back!

More resources:

- The Adventures with the Universe Journal
- The Money Magic monthly membership

Recommended reading:

- *Write to Riches* by my author bestie, Renee Rose
- *The Secret and The Power* by Rhonda Byrne
- *Beyond Positive Thinking* by Dr. Robert Anthony
- *Ask and it is Given* by Abraham Hicks
- *You are A Badass* by Jen Sincero
- *The Success Principles* by Jack Canfield
- *Get Rich, Lucky Bitch* by Denise Duffield-Thomas
- *We Should all be Millionaires* by Rachel Rodgers

Gratitude studies (check out the excellent video "An Antidote to Satisfaction" by Kurzgesagt)

Extra magic Spells

Magic spell

The Gratitude Game: Write out ten things you're grateful for and why you're grateful for them. Feel the feelings of gratitude.

I am so grateful for _____

because _____

_____

I am so grateful for _____

because _____

_____

I am so grateful for _____

because _____

_____

I am so grateful for _____

because _____

_____

I am so grateful for _____

because _____

_____

My love list:

Magic spell

The Gratitude Game: Write out ten things you're grateful for and why you're grateful for them. Feel the feelings of gratitude.

I am so grateful for _____

because _____

_____

I am so grateful for _____

because _____

_____

I am so grateful for _____

because _____

_____

I am so grateful for _____

because _____

_____

I am so grateful for _____

because _____

_____

My love list:

Magic spell

The Gratitude Game: Write out ten things you're grateful for and why you're grateful for them. Feel the feelings of gratitude.

I am so grateful for _____

because _____

_____

I am so grateful for _____

because _____

_____

I am so grateful for _____

because _____

_____

I am so grateful for _____

because _____

_____

I am so grateful for _____

because _____

_____

My love list:

Magic spell

The Gratitude Game: Write out ten things you're grateful for and why you're grateful for them. Feel the feelings of gratitude.

I am so grateful for _____

because _____

_____

I am so grateful for _____

because _____

_____

I am so grateful for _____

because _____

_____

I am so grateful for _____

because _____

_____

I am so grateful for _____

because _____

_____

My love list:

Magic spell

The Gratitude Game: Write out ten things you're grateful for and why you're grateful for them. Feel the feelings of gratitude.

I am so grateful for _____

because _____

_____

I am so grateful for _____

because _____

_____

I am so grateful for _____

because _____

_____

I am so grateful for _____

because _____

_____

I am so grateful for _____

because _____

_____

My love list:

Magic spell

The Gratitude Game: Write out ten things you're grateful for and why you're grateful for them. Feel the feelings of gratitude.

I am so grateful for _____

because _____

_____

I am so grateful for _____

because _____

_____

I am so grateful for _____

because _____

_____

I am so grateful for _____

because _____

_____

I am so grateful for _____

because _____

_____

My love list:

Magic spell

The Gratitude Game: Write out ten things you're grateful for and why you're grateful for them. Feel the feelings of gratitude.

I am so grateful for _____

because _____

_____

I am so grateful for _____

because _____

_____

I am so grateful for _____

because _____

_____

I am so grateful for _____

because _____

_____

I am so grateful for _____

because _____

_____

My love list:

Magic spell

The Gratitude Game: Write out ten things you're grateful for and why you're grateful for them. Feel the feelings of gratitude.

I am so grateful for _____

because _____

_____

I am so grateful for _____

because _____

_____

I am so grateful for _____

because _____

_____

I am so grateful for _____

because _____

_____

I am so grateful for _____

because _____

_____

My love list:

Text copyright © 2023 Silverwood Press, LLC
All Rights Reserved
No part of this book may be reproduced in any form or by any electronic or mechanical means including information storage and retrieval systems, without permission in writing from the author. The only exception is by a reviewer, who may quote short excerpts in a review.
Neither the publisher nor the author shall be held liable or responsible for any loss or damage allegedly arising from any suggestion or information contained in this book.

www.ingramcontent.com/pod-product-compliance
Lightning Source LLC
Chambersburg PA
CBHW052148070526
44585CB00017B/2022